MINDFULNESS FOR BEGINNERS

Ultimate Guide To Achieve Happiness by Eliminating Stress, Depression and Anxiety

Sarah Rowland

Copyright © 2017 by Sarah Rowland

All rights reserved. No part of this book may be reproduced or transmitted in any form or by any means, electronic or mechanical, including photocopying, recording or by any information storage and retrieval system without written permission of the publisher, except for the inclusion of brief quotations in a review.

TABLE OF CONTENTS

Introduction 1

Chapter 1 *The Power Of Mindfulness* 3

    What is Mindfulness? 3

    How Does Mindfulness Help Stress, Anxiety and Depression? .4

    Mindfulness for Other Emotions 7

    Empowering Your Mindfulness Practice 9

Chapter 2 *Simple Practices* 12

    Grounding Technique 12

    Short Body Scan 17

    How Are You Doing? 20

    Mindful Breathing 23

Chapter 3 *Advanced Practices* 28

    Mindful Morning Routine 30

    Mindful Night Time Routine 41

    Every Day Mindfulness 48

    Mindfulness Maintenance Tips 52

Chapter 4 *Digging Deeper* 59

    Getting to the Root Cause.. 60

    Addressing Painful Emotions 64

    The Power of Releasing 69

    When Your Practice Fades..74

Conclusion 80

INTRODUCTION

Mindfulness is a practice that has a powerful ability to teach people to develop a sense of self-awareness and understanding. When you develop a mindfulness practice, you give yourself the opportunity to learn more about your inner self and how you operate with the world around you.

"*Mindfulness for Beginners*: Ultimate Guide to Achieve Happiness by Eliminating Stress, Anxiety, and Depression" is a guide that will teach you how to master mindfulness and take control over your life once and for all. Every day, people suffer from stress, anxiety and depression. The suffering is often prolonged because people are unaware about how they can deal with their own internal responses to these emotions, therefore they attempt to repress them or they take actions which make them worse.

In this guide, you are going to learn how you can master the art and transform your life. While mindfulness will not eliminate the experiences of stress, anxiety and depression, it certainly will help you learn how you can gain control over these emotions and work through them effectively and in a way that serves you.

Throughout this book you are going to learn about the value of mindfulness, as well as be guided through specific strategies that will help you practice mindfulness in your own life. You will learn about instant remedies, maintenance strategies, and larger practices that will help you gain control over problems that run deeper than the day-to-day stuff. Please take your time, relax, read at your own pace, and enjoy!

CHAPTER 1
The Power Of Mindfulness

Mindfulness practices have been taught for decades. The lessons of mindfulness teach us to explore our inner worlds on a deeper level, which provides us with a greater sense of self-awareness. As a result, we learn how to masterfully work together with our emotions to achieve a higher level of peace in life.

What is Mindfulness?

While nearly everyone is talking about it, many people are unclear as to what mindfulness is exactly. In the bigger picture, mindfulness is exactly what you may think: a deeper sense of self-awareness that teaches you all about how you interact with the world around you and within' you.

On a smaller scale, however, mindfulness is many things. It is the series of strategies you use to develop that greater sense of self-awareness. It is also the exact moment when you stop reacting and start recognizing how you feel and the present moment and start responding to it. Mindfulness is an on-going practice that you must work on regularly to maintain it. While you can achieve mindfulness, you cannot maintain it if you don't work towards it. You will have to continually learn to balance yourself in order to achieve mindfulness for a long period of time. Some days it will be easier than others, some days you might feel as though you've failed altogether. The reality is that as long as you are having these regular check ins, then you are doing exactly what you need to be doing to maintain your mindfulness practice.

How Does Mindfulness Help Stress, Anxiety and Depression?

There are three levels where mindfulness assists with reducing and eliminating stress, anxiety and depression. Each of these levels will be available in every instance of the aforementioned emotions, but you might only realize your "window of opportunity" in one of them. They are: before, during, and after. Regardless of where you find your opportunity to start practicing mindfulness, the main point is that you start.

Before

Having a regular, on-going mindfulness maintenance practice can significantly reduce levels of stress, anxiety and depression. Because of your frequent check-ins and practices, you will likely find that you pay greater attention to your body and therefore you are able to deal with certain internal (or external) circumstances before they evolve into anything significant. As a result, you will be able to prevent yourself from having the added stress, anxiety and depression that many people accumulate by ignoring their bodies.

During

People who maintain a regular mindfulness practice are able to recognize when they are experiencing symptoms of stress, anxiety or depression. Because of this, they are able to recognize that these emotions are merely emotional responses to events in life, and that they are not doomed to feeling this way forever. These people are also equipped with tools to assist them with reducing and eliminating these emotions because they are able to practice mindfulness and transition their mind back into a peaceful place by mindfully working through the present emotions.

After

Sometimes, even extremely mindful people may not be able to recognize that they are beginning to experience symptoms of stress, anxiety or depression. Instead, they notice after the symptoms have already been around for a while. This is completely natural and experienced often by people. It does not mean that you have failed or that it is too late. Instead, it means that you simply need to practice your mindfulness strategies and regain control over the situation by developing your peace.

Regardless of when you recognize symptoms of various emotions creeping up on you, the best thing you can do is respond with mindful practices. It is important that you refrain from beating yourself up over not recognizing the symptoms sooner. Over time, you will become more self-aware and eventually it will be easier for you to recognize the symptoms quickly. However, there will always be times where you may struggle more than others. Remember, mindfulness is a practice that must be practiced regularly in order for it to be maintained.

Mindfulness for Other Emotions

Mindfulness is not restricted to only assisting with reducing and eliminating feelings of stress, anxiety and depression. Having a regular mindfulness practice can aid with many different things in life. You can use it to increase peace and happiness in your life. You can also use it to decrease anger, sadness, and other uncomfortable emotions that you will not want to experience for prolonged periods of time.

It is important to understand that mindfulness is not the same as repression. The key is not to identify unwanted emotions and then repress them in order to replace them with wanted emotions. Instead, mindfulness is an indirect approach to effectively deal with the situation. When you are mindful, you are able to gather a large amount of information around your circumstances and use that to your advantage. You can use it to effectively work through emotions you are experiencing by facing them head on and letting yourself heal through them. As a result, you will then be able to experience a greater sense of peace and happiness. Mindfulness is not the practice of replacing emotions, rather it is the practice of working through them.

Empowering Your Mindfulness Practice

It is important to understand how a mindfulness practice should work. The second word of the experience is "practice", because it is something that you need to practice regularly. When you establish a mindfulness practice, you can empower it by spending time enhancing your skill and continuing the exploration of your inner self. The more you invest into your mindfulness practice, the more powerful it will become and the greater value you will gain from it. Mindfulness is not a practice that is meant to be accomplished and then forgotten about. Instead, mindfulness is a lifelong journey where you continually delve deeper into yourself and learn more and more about yourself along the way.

Empowering your mindfulness practice is simple. You simply must believe in it, practice regularly, and allow yourself to nurture it enough so that it will grow. By doing this, you will ensure that you have a strong mindfulness practice that will serve you for years to come. Ideally you should take your favorite mindfulness guides, such as this one, and revisit them from time to time to ensure that you are staying on track with your practice. Guides like this are excellent for beginners as well as those who have been practicing for a long time. Mindfulness is actually a simple practice. However, the longer we practice the more complex we may make it out to be. The best thing you can do is make sure that you are keeping it light and focusing on the foundation of the practice. The rest will take care of itself as a result.

Mindfulness is a powerful practice that allows people to explore the depths of their inner world. When you practice mindfulness, you gain the ability to learn more about yourself than ever before. Instead of reacting to your inner and outer circumstances, you will learn to respond. You will also gain a greater sense of self-awareness that will allow you to know how you feel and think at all times. This means that you will have a greater opportunity to change the way you work together with your own mind and emotions and thus have more control over your life in general. Mindfulness is not a practice that allows you to replace uncomfortable emotions with pleasant ones. Rather, it is a practice that teaches you to effectively work through the painful emotions to open up room in your life for you to welcome the pleasant ones.

CHAPTER 2
Simple Practices

When you are learning mindfulness, it is important to understand simple practices first. Then, you can build your way up from there. Simple practices are practices that take five minutes or less. You should start your journey of mindfulness by practicing one or two of these each day. Additionally, you can use these strategies whenever you recognize that you are having a moment where you are reacting to your circumstances more than you typically do. They will assist you with regathering control over the situation and responding in a way that serves your highest good.

Grounding Technique

Having a solid grounding technique available is important. Grounding allows you to become present in the moment and refrain from magnifying situations in your mind. Many times when we feel excessively emotional about particular things we have a tendency to obsess over them and make them seem bigger or worse than they really are. When you are able to effectively ground yourself from these energies and emotions, you allow yourself the ability to step back and remove yourself from this obsessive reaction. Then, you can respond with actions that will serve your highest good.

You should ground yourself at least twice a day. Once in the morning and once at night. Doing this will help you wake up and shed the stresses of the day before, and will allow you to go to bed after shedding the stresses of the day you had. Grounding is not an opportunity to eliminate unwanted emotions, rather it is an opportunity to remove yourself from the obsessive thinking part and gives you the chance to look at it from a more neutralized state of mind. You should also use your grounding strategy when you are experiencing a heightened sense of emotions that is causing you to check out of the moment and become absorbed in your mind as you obsess over events you cannot control.

To ground yourself, you want to start by standing or sitting somewhere with your feet planted firmly on the floor. Take a few moments to breathe deeply, and then start to check in with your body. You will do this by first checking in with your eyes. Take a moment to notice what your eyes feel like. Are they dry? Do they ache in behind from stress? Are you blinking more than usual? What do you notice? Once you have checked in, take a few moments to look at five things around the room. What five things do you see that catch your eye?

Next, think about your hands. What do your hands feel like? As you are looking at them, how do they look? Notice the edges against whatever background they are against. Then, take a few moments to notice four things you can touch. Don't simply touch these things, but rather take some time to explore them with your hands. What do they feel like? What is the texture? Are they warm or cold? What do you notice about them that is unique or stands out to you most? Take your time and experience each of the four things.

Now you are going to think about your ears. How do they feel? When we are stressed, anxious or depressed, sometimes our ears can feel hot. We may even hear ringing noises or notice that our environment sounds faded out as we are so absorbed in our thoughts. Take a few moments to listen to the things around you. What are three things you can hear? What do they sound like? Are they sounds you hear so often they fade into the background, or are they sounds that are new to you? What else do you notice about the sounds? Give yourself a few moments to really explore each sound and identify everything you can about it.

Next let's move onto your nose. Noses are fascinating. Even though we can see them with our eyes, our eyes are so used to them that they have learned to make them invisible to us so that we can focus on our surroundings past our nose. Take a few seconds to think about how your nose feels on your face. Sometimes when our emotions are particularly uncomfortable we can develop discomfort in our sinuses or regular itching on our faces. Do you notice any of this? If you do, take a few moments to consciously release the tension and discomfort. Then, notice two things you can smell. What are the two things? Where are they coming from? Are they pleasant, or does the smell not appeal to you? Give it a few moments as you really address these questions and recognize how these smells make you feel and where they are coming from.

Finally, we are going to consider your mouth. Take a few moments to really explore your mouth. Is it dry? If so, take a sip of water. Alternatively, do you find that you are holding your tongue in a different position because of your present emotions? Maybe you have it stuck to the roof of your mouth, or maybe you are biting it between your teeth. If so, allow yourself to relax and let your tongue rest again. When you are ready, think about something you can taste right now. If there is no outstanding flavor in your mouth, consider taking a sip of a beverage or a bite of a snack so that you can explore the flavor in your mouth. When you are done, swallow it.

Following these experiences, give yourself a few moments to breathe deeply and really feel your feet as they are planted firmly on the floor. Recognize that you are being supported by the earth and that you are exactly where you need to be in this very moment. When you are feeling relaxed and present again, you can resume your daily activities.

Having a regular grounding routine this way allows you to activate all of your five senses in a matter of minutes. When you are able to do so, you bring your entire awareness back into the present moment. This assists with bringing you out of your mind and can help you stay focused and present in the current situation. If you find that you regularly "check out" of circumstances when you are experiencing certain emotions that may be particularly difficult or uncomfortable, it is a good idea to practice a grounding session. The session doesn't have to be long or intensive, just a few minutes of breathing and focusing on your senses can help you focus your awareness and resume your day from a more mindful state.

Short Body Scan

Short body scans are a quick scan you can do to assess your body for any tension or discomfort. If you notice any, you will want to make sure that you address it quickly and allow it to fade away.

Unlike the full body scan that you will learn in the advanced practices section, this is a quick scan that will allow you to quickly fix anything you are experiencing and move on.

You will want to practice this once per day until you learn how to do the full body scan. Once you learn the full body scan, you can replace this scan with that one. As you are getting started, however, the short body scan is sufficient. You are more than welcome to use this strategy at any time throughout the day, especially if you are experiencing a significant amount of painful or difficult emotions. In some cases, grounding yourself will not be enough and you will need to consciously release specific tensions. For those circumstances, the short body scan is an excellent tool to use.

To start the short body scan, take a few moments to get comfortable and breathe deeply. If you are in a situation where you can't get completely comfortable, simply relax as much as you can and breathe deeply. You may or may not wish to close your eyes depending on where you are. The only thing you will definitely want to have available to you is a few quick moments of silence where you do not have to actively engage with anyone or anything.

As you are breathing deeply, start doing your body scan. Imagine there is a long wand that is horizontal to the ground. The wand starts by hovering slightly above your head, and then moves down the front of you at a slow but steady pace. As it moves down, you can feel the energy moving with it. Anywhere there is tension or discomfort in your body, the wand stops momentarily and zaps it out of you. Then, it carries on as it scans towards your feet. The scan is done when the wand is just below your feet.

If you noticed any tension during this scan, you can either address it immediately or at a more appropriate time. If you are addressing it immediately, use the following instructions. If you are addressing it at a later time, ground yourself for the time being and then return to the discomfort when you have more time to work through the emotions.

To work through the emotions and tension, simply take a few moments to meditate on the discomfort. Work to discover what it is telling you and identify why the discomfort exists in the first place. There are many reasons as to why we feel these discomforts. It may be because you failed to listen to your body, or it may be because you are not working through emotions that are building up inside  of you. Regardless of what it is, take a few moments and identify it. Then, let your body guide you through the process of working it out. You may need to move around and exercise, you may need to rest something or give yourself a total rest, or you may need to simply cry or experience the emotion inside of you so that it can be released and you can move on. Whatever you need to do, give yourself the permission to do it when you are in a safe place and then let yourself work through it. When you are done, you will find that you feel infinitely better as you are no longer harboring the discomfort of ignoring your personal needs.

How Are You Doing?

When you ask someone how they are doing, you are prompting them to quickly check in with themselves and then provide you with an answer. While they may automatically answer "good"

thinking that's what you want to hear, it still encourages them to take a moment to think about how they are actually doing. Often, we forget to ask ourselves how we are doing and as a result our needs go unheard. It is important to establish the type of relationship with yourself where you aren't afraid to ask yourself how you are doing on a regular basis.

This practice is an extremely quick one that should be completed regularly throughout the day. You can do it first thing in the morning, last thing at night, and frequently throughout the day. The more you ask yourself how you are doing, the more you will be able to check in with yourself and treat yourself appropriately.

There is no real set up for this mindfulness strategy. You will not need to practice any deep breathing beforehand. Rather, you simply need to say "Hey, how are you doing?" to yourself. You might wish to do it in a mirror, or you might simply wish to quietly or mentally ask yourself the question. Do in a way that feels comfortable for you. Then, allow yourself to genuinely answer the question. Based on whatever your answers are, you can take the appropriate action to manage the situation. If you are genuinely feeling good, then there is no further action required. However, if you are feeling stressed, anxious, depressed, hungry, uncomfortable, tired, or any other unpleasant emotion, you can use this as an opportunity to choose a solution and work with yourself to achieve a better overall state.

Asking yourself how you are doing forces you to take a moment to really consider how you are actually doing. If you find it's difficult to come up with an answer, then simply adjust your questions. Ask: "Hey heart, how are you doing?" and then consider your emotional state. Are you feeling comfortable or uncomfortable? Then, ask "hey mind, how are you doing?" and allow yourself to answer that question. Is your mind at peace, or is something troubling you? Next, ask yourself "hey body, how are you doing?" and consider your body for a moment. Is your body feeling energized and functional, or is there tension or pain being carried somewhere within' you? Finally, ask "hey soul, how are you doing?" and consider that for a moment. Are there any wanted, hopes, dreams or spiritual needs going unmet? Once you get the answer to each question, take a few minutes to generate a solution so that you can resolve the problem. Then, you can take action on the resolution and move forward feeling more whole and at peace with yourself.

Mindful Breathing

Sometimes when we are feeling out of control with our emotions or thoughts the best thing we can do is take a moment and breathe through it. With stress and anxiety especially, the answer isn't always to bring yourself back into the present moment immediately. Instead, you want to take a few minutes to breathe it out. If you are experiencing a heightened level of stress or anxiety, take a few minutes to breathe it out. You will find that you are feeling much better afterwards.

Deep breathing is a great daily exercise, and it is involved in almost all of the other mindfulness practices. If you desire, you can add deep breathing as an activity all on its own. It can help you generate peace and calmness within' your body which provides you with an excellent foundation for practicing mindfulness techniques. If you choose to add it to your daily routine, spend a few minutes before your daily practices working with your breath. You should also follow your daily practices with the breathing technique.

Breathing is simple, we do it every day all day long. Whether we realize it or not, we are breathing. Turning breathing into a mindfulness practice is extremely simple and mainly requires you to bring your awareness to your breath.

You want to start by simply becoming aware of your breath. Don't try and manipulate it or change it in any way. Instead, simple take a moment to notice every time you breathe in and out. Try and become aware over how long each breath lasts and what you feel like as you are breathing. Can you identify where the breath is being stored? Are you breathing into your throat, lungs, or belly? Let yourself become aware over your own breath for about 30 breaths or one minute.

Once you are aware of your natural breath, take a few moments to start adjusting it. Breathe in just a little longer each time, and breathe out just a little longer each time. Continue lengthening the process until each breath feels deep and relaxing. Make sure you are breathing into your diaphragm and not your chest as it will make you feel even more relaxed.

Science shows that when we are stressed our breath shallows and when we are relaxed our breath deepens. As a result, when we control our breath to be deeper and slower, our body will naturally relax with the breath. You can use this as an opportunity to eliminate stress and difficult emotions and welcome relaxation and peace into your life. Use this technique any time you need to draw stress out of your life and infuse it with peace and calmness.

Short mindfulness practices are powerful for helping you cope with day-to-day activities. You can use these practices to establish your beginner-level daily routine. Each one will allow you to begin building the foundation for your overall mindfulness practice and will give you the opportunity to truly start exploring your inner self. Remember, even though mindfulness practices are generally the same from one person to the next, your own journey will differ based on your unique life events and circumstances. Your past, present, and inner being will all shape the way you experience the world around you. As a result, your response to mindfulness practices and to life itself will be unique to you. Try not to judge yourself based on how you deal with things or compare yourself to others based on how they deal with things. This journey is your own and you should take the time to genuinely embrace it and learn as much about yourself as you possibly can.

When you are in the process of moving forward to advanced techniques, don't feel the need to erase the short techniques. While these techniques will alter to become a part of your daily routine, you should continue to keep them in your mindfulness toolbox as remedies for your day-to-day experiences. If you experience discomforts in the office, while driving, at home, in the supermarket, or anywhere else these tools are excellent to help you come back to the present moment and respond in your chosen manner. These tools are excellent for when you need something in a pinch and don't have several minutes to go through an elaborate routine to bring yourself back to the room. Remember, when the short practices begin to be used as remedies throughout the day you are not using them as an opportunity to repress emotions that you do not want to experience. Rather, you use them to bring yourself back to the room and move your emotions and difficulties to the side until you can face them head on. When you return to your daily routines, be sure to take advantage of the opportunity to bring those emotions back to the surface and work through them efficiently. By bringing them back and working through them properly, you give yourself the ability to truly eliminate them instead of leaving them to build up and become a greater problem later on.

CHAPTER 3
Advanced Practices

While you do not want to rush into the advanced mindfulness practices, eventually you are going to need to venture beyond the short practices. Advanced mindfulness practices give you the opportunity to elaborate on your short practices and establish a more sustainable routine that will enable you to maintain your mindfulness for years to come.

As mentioned in the previous chapter, don't erase the short practices completely. Instead, use them as remedies for day-to-day experiences and bring yourself back to these emotions during the following routines to help you work through them effectively.

You will notice that the advanced practices are actually routines instead of simple practices. That is because routines encourage your mind and body to respond in certain ways. Therefore, having actual routine practices in place means that when you begin the routine your mind will be conditioned to respond to it in the most effective way possible. As a result, you will be able to easily bring yourself into a mindful state and work through anything you need to work through.

The following practices include a morning routine, a night time routine, individual practices you should be using throughout the day, and tips to help you maintain your mindfulness effectively. These are the strategies you will use on a more regular basis to keep your mindfulness practice strong, so take your time and begin to get to know them really well. If you need to, you can adjust some of the practices to suit your needs better.

When you are in the process of transitioning from beginner to advance, you will want to do so slowly. Start by adding a morning routine, then a night time routine. Then, you can start adding the daily practices and utilizing the tips to keep everything flowing smoothly. There is no need to rush into the switch. In fact, the slower you take it, the faster everything will stick and you will be able to comfortably use it for years to come. Remember, take everything at your own pace and be mindful over your own desires and needs. If you need to alter something or switch up the order in which things are done, then it is more effective to do so then it is to avoid it and make the practice uncomfortable for you as a result.

Mindful Morning Routine

In order to truly master your mindfulness practice, you will want to have a regular morning routine in place. Morning routines allow you to start your day out with the right frame of mind in order to tackle the rest of your day from a mindful perspective. Of course, you will still need to check in and refresh that perspective. However, starting your day out right can minimize the number of refreshers you will need throughout the day.

There are a few important elements to a mindful morning routine. The following steps will guide you through the process of an ideal routine. Of course, you can adjust yours to fit your needs better. Remember, we all learn and grow in different ways, so feel free to make any adjustments you need in order to achieve the maximum benefit from your own practice.

First Breaths

When you first wake in the morning, you may feel compelled to jump out of bed and head to the bathroom. Although it is satisfying to relieve yourself after a long night's sleep, it can also have you feeling a little rattled first thing in the morning. Instead of leaping out of bed, try starting your first mindful practice of the day.

Your first breaths of the day should be wholesome and relaxing. Take a few moments to take three deep, refreshing breaths. Ultimately, you want to hold fast to those relaxing breaths we take as we are asleep. Allow your body to breathe naturally, but also allow for it to stay in a relaxed state. Don't manipulate the breath to become shallow or fast by feeling a rush to get up. There is no need to prolong this practice. Simply allow yourself to become mindful over your breath for the first three breaths of your morning. When you are done, you can rise from bed and prepare yourself for the rest of your day. Make sure you relieve yourself, and then have a nice large glass of cool water before moving on to the rest of the mindfulness routine.

Gratitude

When you express gratitude first thing in the morning, you set the tone for the rest of the day. Your mindset will be calm and pure, and you will naturally start looking for the wonderful aspects of your day. Gratitude practices are taught in virtually every mindfulness lesson because they have such a powerful impact on the way you live your life. It can certainly pay off to listen to the advice and start implementing your own gratitude practice throughout the day.

There are many ways that you can implement a gratitude practice into your life. Depending on what feels comfortable for you, you may wish to say it out loud, think it quietly in your mind, or write it down in a journal. It does not matter what way you choose, as long as it feels satisfying to you.

Before you start expressing gratitude, take a few moments to take a deep breath. Try and challenge yourself to dig deeper. Of course, expressing gratitude for anything is important, but often we get caught up in expressing it for obvious things: cars, money, friends, luxuries, and more. While you should certainly express gratitude for these things, try and challenge yourself to pick five things that you may not normally think about. For example, the pen you are writing with, the sun visor in your car, the bulb in your lamp, so on and so forth. When you start to look more closely at what you have, you learn to appreciate things more deeply. Often we become oblivious to just how much we have in life. Mindfulness practices such as this allow you to learn how you can look more critically at the world around you and truly see exactly what you have and offer appreciation for it.

Mindful Meditation

Each morning routine should have some form of mindfulness meditation involved. How long you choose to meditate for is unique to you, but the average recommended time is between 5 and 15 minutes. Anything longer than 15 minutes is not entirely necessary.

In order to practice your mindful meditation in the morning, start by sitting in a comfortable position and closing your eyes. Then, you can start focusing on your breath. There is no need to manipulate or control your breath, simply focus on it. Once you are focused on your breath, hold your focus there for a while. If you notice that your attention is wandering, take a moment and gently guide it back to your breath. It is natural for your attention to wander, especially so early in the morning. Never punish yourself for this. Instead, simply acknowledge what has happened and draw your awareness back.

Mindful meditation is a powerful practice that can help bring you into the present moment in a gentle way. You should include meditation in your mindfulness morning routine even if you choose to adjust this routine in any way. If you struggle to gauge the amount of time that you have been meditating for, set an alarm on your phone for 5 to 15 minutes from the moment you start. Then, you can simply focus on your breath and trust that you will know when to stop when the alarm rings.

Body Scan

Conducting a body scan first thing in the morning is important. After a long night of sleep we can often wake up with residual tension. They may be tensions that we hold on to from sleep, or they may be tensions that we hold on to from the day before. Regardless of where they come from, taking a moment to identify them and work through them can help eliminate them as you carry on to tackle the rest of your day.

If you desire, you can move directly from your meditation into your body scan. Alternatively, you may wish to adjust yourself and then get comfortable again for the body scan. That is entirely up to you.

To start your body scan you want to be relaxed and have your eyes closed. Ideally you should be sitting or lying down in a position that is open and loose. You do not want to be clenching anything, tucking anything in, or otherwise creating your own bodily discomforts. The more relaxed and loosened your body is, the better. Once you are relaxed, take a moment to start mindfully scanning through your body parts. Start with the crown of your head, down your forehead and the back of your skull, and through the middle. Take a moment to notice your ears, eyes, and nose. Then, move down to the cheeks, mouth, and jaw. If you notice any tension or discomfort in these areas, take a few moments to focus upon that area and send it love. See if you can discover anything about this area and find out why there is discomfort being held there. If you can find out why, take a mental note so that you can resolve this issue going forward. For example, if your jaw is tense from stress at work, your resolve may be to reduce the stress you experience at work by increasing your mindfulness practice and allowing yourself to release emotions at the end of the day.

After scanning your head, move down to your neck and shoulders. Then, move down your arms into your biceps and triceps, down through your elbows and into your forearms. Finally, scan your wrists, palms, and fingers all the way to the tips. Again, if you notice any discomfort in any of these areas, take a few moments to send love to it and see if you can discover what the issue appears to be.

Next, you want to scan your chest, down through your torso and into your waist. Take some time noticing your pelvic bone and your hips, then move down through your glutes and into your thighs. Then, you can scan down to your knees, through your calves, and into your ankles and feet. End your scan by moving your awareness all the way through your toes. As you may suspect, if you notice any tension or discomfort in these areas take some time to send love and awareness to the area and do your best to identify the root cause of the problem.

Daily body scans allow you to check in with your body and recognize anything that may be going on. If there is any discomfort, tension, or other unwelcomed feelings you want to take the time to become aware of these things. When you do, you give yourself the ability to recognize what your body needs and give it what it is asking for. If you do not respect your body when it asks for what it needs, the problem will grow until the point where it is unavoidable. It is best to get in control of everything ahead of time rather than waiting for it to get worse and then wishing you had dealt with it sooner. As a result of taking care of your body in this way, you will notice that it starts to feel healthier and better overall. Because of this, you will feel a greater sense of peace and happiness because you will not be physically uncomfortable or at dis-ease.

Check In

After a thorough body scan it is a great time to check in with your emotional self. Take this opportunity to ask yourself how you are feeling. Then, take a moment to notice what answers come up for you.

When you are doing this practice, it is a good idea to have your journal handy. Writing down what comes up for you can help you work through it. You might notice a trend over a few days if you have an issue that is particularly difficult for you. Additionally, writing it down can give you a different perspective on the situation which can assist you with working through it.

Your check in process doesn't have to take long. Simply ask yourself how you are doing and then allow yourself to honestly answer the question. Some days you might find that you are doing well, others you might find that you are struggling with a particular set of emotions. Either way, it is important to know so that you can keep in touch with your emotional body and nurture it the same way you would want to nurture your physical body if anything were to be wrong with it.

Mindful Breathing

Finally, you want to wrap up your morning routine with a mindful breathing practice. Once again, take a few moments to bring your awareness to your breath. This time you are going to want to be mindful of ten full breaths. There is no need to manipulate these breaths to be longer or shorter, deeper or more shallow. You can simply become aware of how your body is naturally breathing in this very moment.

Once you have completed your ten breaths, you are done your morning routine! The entire process should take you no longer than about half an hour, depending on how long you choose to take in order to complete each practice. After completing a powerful morning routine, you will likely feel a lot better about starting your entire day. Often times we take minimum care of our bodies in the morning. We relieve ourselves, slam a glass of water, eat some breakfast, jump in the shower, dress ourselves and then run out the door. When we rush through the motions this way and fail to actually take care of our body the way it needs to be cared for, we set ourselves up for failure. A body that is being ignored is a body that does not perform at its peak function. If your body is failing to perform at its peak function, it is because you are not nurturing it the way it needs to be. Your body will always tell you what it needs, all you need to do is take a moment to turn into the silence and listen. When you do this, you give yourself the opportunity to care for yourself in the best way possible and as a result your body will serve you to its highest ability.

Mindful Night Time Routine

In addition to a powerful mindful morning routine, you need to have a powerful mindful night time routine as well. The night time routine will allow you to shed the stress of the day and truly prepare yourself for bed time so that you can have a restful sleep that will provide you with the ability to have a wonderful morning.

Most people report that their largest concern is fatigue and a lack of sleep. Many times, even if you are getting the appropriate hours of sleep per night, your sleep is not high quality because you are not relieving yourself from stress and tension before bed. As a result, you suffer from low sleep quality because your body simply cannot rest deeply enough. Your physical, psychological and emotional bodies will all suffer from your lack of attention, which can be extremely difficult to endure especially after a prolonged period of time.

The best night time routine is simple, relaxing, and takes very little time. This routine takes about 20-30 minutes for you to complete and it ends with you getting into your bed. Because of that, you want to make this the last thing you do before you sleep. If you do this too early in the night you may open yourself up to receive more stress and tension before bed which will ultimately negate from the benefit of this practice.

Mindful Breathing and Grounding

The first thing you want to do when you are starting your night time routine is practice mindful breathing and ground yourself. Start with the breathing. You can do this by taking a few deep breaths and drawing your awareness into each breath. Once your attention is rested upon your breath, take about 10 more breaths. Notice the way each breath feels. Take some time to recognize which areas of your body are affected by the breath. You can also become aware of what your natural breathing is like in that moment, and notice if it changes over the course of the ten breaths.

Once you are in total awareness of your breath, shift your focus to the floor beneath your feet. Become aware of how it supports your feet no matter where you are. At any time in your life you can rest your feet firmly on the floor and it will support you no matter where you are, what you are doing, or how you are feeling. Next, bring your attention to the surface that your body is rested upon. Notice how your body feels as it settles into the support.

Finally, start looking at the room around you. Notice anything that stands out for you. If you see anything new, take some time to notice that. If there are any sounds that are standing out to you, really become aware about those as well. Take a few seconds to notice what they are and how they affect the way you feel and think about the present moment.

After you are completely grounded, move into a body scan.

Body Scan

As with all of the previous body scans, this body scan is going to enable you to look through your entire body and notice anywhere that may be holding tension or discomfort. Doing this after you are grounded will ensure that you do not spend this time fixated on other concerns from your daily experiences. You can do this scan in your bed so that you are ready for sleep afterward.

This time your body scan is going to be slightly different. You are going to relax and imagine as though there is a gold light moving through your body. As the light fills more of you up any tension, stress, negativity or discomfort will be displaced until finally it is pushed out of your body completely.

Start by relaxing and imagining that there is a golden light above your head. As you notice it, notice that it starts slowly moving towards the crown of your head. Already, you can feel yourself relaxing as it nears your body. Once it penetrates the crown of your head, imagine it moving down through your entire skull and face, washing through to your neck and shoulders. Any tension that may be built up in your head or jaw is being pushed out of place with the light as it moves down through your neck and shoulders, then all the way down your arms. If there is any tension in your arms, imagine it is being pushed out of the end of your fingertips until there is none left and both of your arms are completely filled with the golden light. Return your awareness back to your chest and picture the light pushing down through your chest. It moves down through your abdomen towards your hips, pressing everything down your body. Then it moves through your glutes, thighs, knees and calves. Finally, it moves through your ankles and feet, pushing any remaining discomfort, stress, negativity or tension out through the bottoms of your feet.

Once you are done the scan, take a few moments to really picture your body glowing with this golden light. Every ounce of tension and discomfort has been removed from your body and all that remains is the beautiful golden healing energy that allows you to feel deeply relaxed and comfortable in the moment. Any tension that was not directly dealt with can be focused on in your morning routine. Now is not the time to work through the tensions, but rather to melt them away so that you can relax. They can be dealt with at a later time.

Instead of coming out of this meditative state, simply move on to the mindful meditation practice.

Mindful Meditation

Now that you are already relaxed from your body scan, it is a great time to move on to your mindful meditation. After you are done imagining the golden light, take a few moments to bring your awareness to your breath. Notice how deep or shallow it is, how frequently you are breathing, and what parts of your body are being affected by the breath.

This time, there is no need to set an alarm as you are simply going to meditate until right before you fall asleep. Make sure you don't meditate until you pass out because this can lead to the unwanted habit of you falling asleep every time you try to meditate, rather than you actually effectively meditating.

Acknowledge the breath for as long as you comfortably can. At night, we have a tendency to let our minds wander. If you notice this is happening, bring your attention back to your breath. Do not punish yourself for this, rather gently bring back your attention. Eventually, it will be significantly easier for you to stay entirely focused on the meditation process. Practice your meditation until you are just about to pass out.

One Last Stretch

Before you are about to fall asleep and after you finish your meditation, take a moment to stretch yourself out one last time. Start with your feet and toes, stretch them out completely and then tighten them up. Release your tension and let your feet relax completely. Next, stretch out your legs and then clench them. After a moment, release the clench and let them relax completely. Now you want to do this same patter for your glutes, your abdomen, your hands, your arms, your chest, and your shoulders. Finally, do it for your neck, jaw, and face. When you are done, your entire body should feel completely relaxed.

Final Breaths

Just before you pass out, take three mindful breaths. Notice how your entire body feels, notice where your breath is at, and notice what it feels like to be breathing in that pattern. When you are done, you can close your eyes and fall asleep.

Having a night time routine like this can teach you to release the tension from the day and enter a peaceful state of mind before bed. It gives you the opportunity to relax entirely so that when you rest you have a deep sleep. People who do not mindfully release their daily tension often go to bed stressed out and as a result they have poor sleep quality. They end up living in a constant state of fatigue because they are not sleeping well, even if they are sleeping an adequate number of hours per night. Many other ailments can arise from poor sleep quality, which you do not want to experience. Having this routine in place, or a similar routine, will allow you to get a high quality rest so that you are able to feel alert and awake the next day.

Every Day Mindfulness

In addition to morning and night time routines, you want to have practices you use throughout the day as well. In the "simple practices" chapter, you were taught a variety of powerful mini-strategies that enable you to maintain control over your mindfulness practice throughout the day. You should continue using those strategies in order to maintain your day-to-day mindfulness practice.

In case you have forgotten which practices those were, they included:

- Grounding Technique
- Short Body Scan
- How Are You Doing?
- Mindful Breathing

In addition to these simple practices, there are a few other areas in which you can infuse your life with mindfulness. They include:

Eating

When you are eating, make sure you are taking some time to truly absorb the experience of your meal. Chew slowly, really notice each flavor in your meal, and take your time in between bites. When you feel satisfied, do not force yourself to eat more. Do not rush yourself, and do not treat it as a chore. Instead, truly experience the process. You will likely learn a lot about yourself and your preferences during this process.

Often, we treat eating like a chore. We go to drive-thru restaurants or we eat convenience meals and we leave out the experience of cooking and preparing our meal. We don't get the experience of plating it and truly looking at it before we eat it because we are in such a rush to eat it as quickly as possible and resume our busy lifestyles. Instead of doing this, make the entire process a mindfulness practice. Take your time when you are preparing the meal, plate it carefully in a way that looks attractive to you, and take your time eating it. Your health will improve significantly as well, as you will not be over eating or indulging in unhealthy food choices anymore.

Listening

It is common that we listen only for the purpose of responding. We never truly hear everything the other person is saying, rather we hear enough to formulate a response and then we stop listening as deeply. Doing this is ineffective as it can lead to misunderstandings and you not absorbing all of the information from the conversation. Instead of listening merely to respond, listen simply to listen. Respond afterwards, when you have received all of the information and have had a moment to thoughtfully think it over.

Listen to each word the person says, and pay attention to their body language as well. Notice what signs they are giving you based on their facial expressions and hand gestures, as well as their posture. Take some time to acknowledge the feelings they are putting into the conversation. When you listen this way, you absorb the entire message that is being offered by the speaker. Then, you can respond in a manner that is truly productive to the conversation. Additionally, you can learn a great deal of knowledge this way.

Speaking and Thinking

The way we speak and think is often uncensored. Many times, we think and say things that are toxic to ourselves or the world around us. We think or speak judgmentally and tear down others and ourselves along the way. As a result, we infuse our lives with a great deal of negativity because we fail to think before we speak.

Instead of simply saying or thinking the first thing that comes to your mind, take a moment to become aware of the thought. Notice what the tone is. Is it judgmental, or is it positive? Will it hurt if it is thought or spoken? Or can it add genuine value?

Thoughts that are deemed negative, hurtful, or otherwise unproductive should be mindfully released in favor of ones that are positive and productive. This way, you are only using your mind power and words to add positivity to the world.

Mindfulness Maintenance Tips

Practicing mindfulness may be difficult for some people. The following is a variety of tips that can help you add depth to your practice and gain the most out of it.

Triggers

Having "triggers" that remind you to check in with yourself is a great way to start practicing mindfulness throughout the day. When you are learning to implement mindfulness into your daily activities it can be difficult, especially never having done it before. Triggers can be any number of things that, when you notice them, you are triggered to remember that you want to practice mindfulness in that moment.

So, imagine your trigger was a clock. Any time you saw a clock you would be triggered to ask "how am I doing?" and then choose a solution based on the answer. Over time you will become so used to asking yourself how you are doing that it will come naturally, whether you see the trigger or not. You will also develop a sense of awareness about yourself that will enable you to know exactly what you need in order to feel better in moments of discomfort which will allow you to promptly resolve any issues that arise.

Triggers can be virtually anything. You may choose a clock, a pen, a specific car, a certain number, a certain word, or anything else. Whatever you choose is completely up to you. Choose something that you will see on a regular basis and then consciously decide that any time you see that item you will remember to ask yourself how you are doing.

At first, you may forget to act on the trigger. However, you will have some form of reaction to the trigger simply because your mind will remember "hey, there was something about clocks that I was supposed to remember". That simple reaction is a great start. Quickly, you will know exactly what the clock is meant to trigger and you will remember to ask the question. It takes time, so be patient with yourself and give it time to sink in.

Journaling

Journaling is a wonderful tool to add to your mindfulness practice. While it may not be ideal to journal everything throughout the entire day, using journaling for larger practices (such as your morning and night time routines) is a great idea.

Your journal can serve you in many ways. First, you can use your journal to write down any experiences that you may be having or any responses you have to certain questions. You can also use it to express gratitude for things in your life. As you are writing all of this down, you are also tracking all of your growth in your mindfulness practice. Any time you want, you can flip back through your pages and notice just how far you have come since you started.

It is a good idea to keep a pen and your journal handy near the spot where you generally practice your morning and night time routines. That way, you can journal on a regular basis and keep track of everything that comes up for you.

Setting Alarms

If triggers aren't enough or you are struggling to remember the purpose of the trigger, you might consider using alarms as well. In your phone, you can set an alarm for every hour that alerts you asking "How are you doing?" That way, you are prompted to check in with yourself on an hourly basis.

Over time, the alarm will serve you in two ways. First, it will teach you to practice mindfulness every hour so that you can stay in touch with yourself and how you are doing. Second, it will turn your phone notifications into a trigger. You will come to expect that notifications on your phone mean that you are being reminded to check in with yourself, therefore any notification you get will remind you to ask yourself how you are doing. It's a wonderful win-win situation!

Making it Personal

The final most important thing you should do when you are developing your mindfulness practice is to make it personal. A mindfulness practice that is copied directly from a book or a guide is one that will likely not mirror exactly what you need. In the beginning, following the guide exactly is a great idea. Over time, however, you will likely identify areas that could serve you better if they were adjusted. Feel confident that if you make these adjustments, your mindfulness practice will serve you even better.

The practice of mindfulness is a highly personal one. It is a journey of your inner self, one that only you can experience. You may be able to share the story with others, but only you can have the true experience yourself. Because of that, only you know exactly what you need from your experience in order for it to serve your highest good. When you adjust your mindfulness practices to reflect these needs, you strengthen it and empower it to serve you in a way that will keep your practice incredibly successful and allow you to master your own mindfulness.

Advancing your mindfulness practice is important. Although you may settle into a sort of routine with your practice, you will likely notice that even the routine is adjusted several times over throughout your life. Your needs and present states of being are constantly changing and therefore your mindfulness practice will constantly change as well. The practices in this section are for you to learn how to transition from a beginner's level to an advanced level of mindfulness practice. From here, it is up to you to continue developing your practice and evolving it into what it needs to be in order to serve your highest good. If you ever feel stuck or as though your practice is fading, return to this chapter and start following it exactly once again. Doing this will refresh your mind and bring you back into the center of your practice, allowing you to continue evolving it for your greater good.

CHAPTER 4
Digging Deeper

Daily practices and maintenance routines are important, but they cannot always resolve large issues. When you are new to mindfulness, you may find that you have a particularly high amount of stress, anxiety, depression or other discomfort that is ailing you. As well, you may find that at certain times in your life there are events that strike a major outbreak of discomfort and pain. For these circumstances, even advanced maintenance practices aren't always enough to help you work through the entire problem.

For this purpose, you are going to explore the digging deeper section. You will be guided through the process of getting to the source of the problem and then eliminating it entirely. In doing so, you will effectively release unwanted discomfort without repressing it in a way that leads to greater discomfort. Ultimately, it is one of the healthiest ways for you to work through anything that ails you. Of course, if you are struggling significantly you should seek professional assistance so that you can resolve anything you may be suffering with. Mindfulness is merely a tool and not a total healing treatment. If you are having great difficulty getting through a hard time, it is highly recommended that you allow a professional to assist you through and use mindfulness as an additional tool for the process.

Getting to the Root Cause

The first part of the process is getting to the root cause of the deep-set discomfort. Depending on what it is, you may not actually know exactly what event caused you to get the discomfort. So, if you can't identify the exact event you at least want to identify the exact emotion. For example, stress may actually be grief, anger, or feeling as though you have not spoken your truth. The clearer you get about what the actual problem is, the more effective you will be in dealing with it.

You can get to the root of these emotions and discomforts by practicing a mindfulness meditation that allows you to truly explore the feeling itself. In doing so, you will learn a great deal about the discomfort and why it exists in the first place. For this meditation, you will want to be in a calm space, and you may wish to have music on. You will then want to be sitting or lying down in a comfortable position that will allow you to meditate without falling asleep.

Start by bringing your awareness to your breath and your body. For now, put the discomfort out of your mind completely. You want to bring your mind into a meditative state that will allow you to tune into your body and become totally aware of the discomfort you are experiencing. To do this, focus on your breath for about 20-30 breaths. When you start to feel relaxed, that is when you want to stop counting and simply maintain your focus on your breath. Take stress and anticipation away and simply spend a few moments appreciating your breath and body.

Once you are completely relaxed, you can start to focus in on the areas that you are feeling the tension or discomfort. Start with just one area. Don't try and manipulate the discomfort in any way, simply bring your awareness to the discomfort. Notice where it is, what it is affecting, and how much it is affecting you. Does the pain feel significant, or small but persistent? At this time, you simply want to identify all of the feelings you are having around the discomfort. If you can, ask the discomfort where it has come from and see if any answers come up for you. Try and understand the discomfort itself and where you have acquired it from.

Once you are more aware about the discomfort itself, how it's affecting you and where it might be coming from, you can simply start to send love to it. The purpose of getting to the root cause is not to alter the discomfort, but rather to understand it more. You are validating the discomfort, becoming aware of its presence and purpose. Following your mindfulness meditation around the discomfort, you can use the root cause as your basis for making necessary changes in your life to prevent it from getting worse and reduce the discomfort as it is. These changes vary greatly. You may simply need to sleep more at night to reduce headaches from tiredness, or you may need to nurture yourself more as you work to reduce heartache from grief. The process does not come from directly eliminating the source but rather understanding it and giving yourself the space to properly work through it so that you can move past it.

It is vital that you remember that the purpose is never to completely distinguish discomfort or unwanted emotions by repressing them or "putting them aside". Instead, you want to get to the root source and genuinely work through it. That way the ailment is completely resolved and you can move forward to carry on with your life, knowing you are at peace with the issue itself.

During your meditation where you are beginning to address the root cause, you may wish to spend a significant amount of time sending love to the discomfort. In doing so, you are validating the emotion and feeling and giving yourself the space to work through what you need to work through in order to move past the discomfort.

Addressing Painful Emotions

There are many times in life where we may encounter painful emotions. Often times we naturally want to repress these emotions because facing them can be extremely difficult. Feeling the painful emotions as they are can feel even more painful, so it can be easy to want to avoid them. When you avoid them, however, you make the pain worse. You end up feeling the pain significantly more in the long run, as well as many other symptoms that arise as a result of this pain being repressed for so long. The better thing to do is to mindfully work through the emotions.

There are many ways that you can mindfully work through emotions, but it is important to note that every way will require you to take the time to actually work through the emotions. The first part of working through difficult emotions is identifying exactly what they are. It can take some time, but you need to really recognize what you are experiencing. For example, are you stressed because of work, or are you experiencing residual anger from a previous argument and therefore taking the emotional burden to work, thus causing your work to be stressful?

Identifying exactly what is causing the difficult emotions is what will allow you to genuinely work through them. While you will want to work through all of the symptoms as well, it is important that you start with the primary purpose.

At first, you may not know what the primary reason is. If that is the case, start with what you think is the primary reason. Through that work, you will likely discover what the actual purpose of the difficult emotions are. With the emotions you are working through, you will want to follow these steps in order to effectively work through them.

The first thing you want to do is to really get clear on what the emotion is and where it came from. It can be beneficial to journal through this process. Start by writing down what you are feeling and why you think you are feeling it. From there, continue writing about what emotions you are feeling and any symptoms you are experiencing as a result. Don't think about what you are writing, simply continue writing about everything that comes into your mind. You will likely discover many more emotions or feelings through this writing exercise that will be brought to light when you stop thinking and start exploring what you are feeling inside.

After you have done this writing exercise, you can start identifying what the primary emotions and symptoms are that you are experiencing. Then, you should give yourself space to work through them. This part of the process may look different for everyone. Depending on what emotion you are experiencing, you may have a different way that you need to work through it. For example, if you are feeling grief you may wish to cry. If you are feeling anger, you may wish to go for a jog or punch a punching bag to release your energy. Depending on what you are feeling, you will want to experience it.

It is important that you work through the emotions in a way that feels right to you. You will likely already have an idea of what you need to do in order to work through your emotions. Something will likely have been lingering in your mind, encouraging you to work through the emotions in a specific way. If you have been having these encouraging feelings, you should take the time to explore them and see how the results make you feel.

It is important that you understand the purpose of emotions. Being mindful about the reason why we experience emotions can allow you to mindfully approach your emotions and reduce your tendency to push them down.

Emotions are feelings that we experience as a result of our life events. We experience many emotions on a day-to-day basis, varying in degrees. The emotions can be pleasurable, or they can be uncomfortable. They can change rapidly, and they can be hard to ignore. The reason behind this is because emotions virtually always bring about a lesson, breakthrough, or deeper understanding of our inner self.

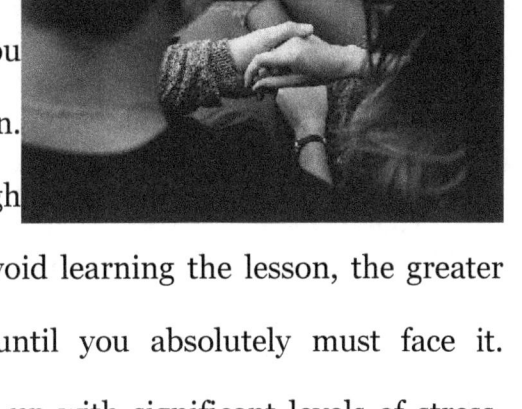

When an emotion is being experienced to serve a lesson, there is only one way that you can actually solve the emotion. That is, you must go through the lesson. The more you avoid learning the lesson, the greater the emotion will become until you absolutely must face it. Alternatively, you may wind up with significant levels of stress, anxiety, depression, or other unwanted emotions. Lessons are generally hard and can push us to step outside of our comfort zone. For example, you may have to speak up for yourself or initiate a confrontation that is outside of what you would typically be comfortable doing. The process of actually speaking up or initiating the confrontation may be extremely difficult but once you complete the task there will be a rewarding experience at the end. This "feel good" experience that you have when you have done something difficult like this is the result of successfully navigating your way through a life lesson.

Breakthroughs are generally what we experience when we have been faced with a life lesson that we have regularly ignored or avoided. When we ignore or avoid life lessons, we no longer experience a simple passing through when we accomplish the lesson. Instead, we often experience what is known as a breakthrough. This means that when you get through to the other side, a large majority of your life will shift for the better. Parts of your life that you have been shrinking and neglecting in order to avoid the lesson will be a part of your breakthrough and you will have a total transformation in your life and psyche as a result.

When we experience deep emotions that are connected to understanding ourselves better, generally the only thing we need to do is experience the emotion. We will learn a great deal about ourselves as a result. You may learn how you naturally respond to various emotions, you may learn about what causes you to experience these emotions, or you may learn about any other number of things. The only way to explore this deeper version of yourself is to actually experience the emotions.

Regardless of why you are experiencing emotions in your life, you need to work through them. The best way is to write down the emotion and let yourself free write as you further explore the emotion. Once you have explored it this way, you can then allow yourself some space and freedom to actually feel your way through the emotion.

The Power of Releasing

Learning to release things is important. Many times you may find that you have worked through emotions but due to poor coping skills you wind up replaying the emotions over and over in your mind. Often this means that you haven't fully worked through the emotion, but other times it can be because you fail to release things after you are done working through them. Effectively releasing things when you are done working through them is an important way to put them in the past and let them go.

The best way that you can release something is to meditate and consciously let it go. Start by breathing deeply and relaxing yourself until you are in a meditative state. Then, you can draw your awareness into your mind's eye. Imagine as though you are walking down a flight of stairs. Take them one stair at a time, genuinely experiencing each stair as you move. Once you get to the bottom, you will notice that there is a door there. You can enter the door and walk through. Behind the door there will be a large, warm, comfy chair that is waiting for you. When you see the chair, you can sit in it and begin to relax.

After you are relaxed in the chair, you can start imagining anything that is causing you severe discomfort. Picture a thought bubble that rises above your head and fill the bubble with everything that ails you. Anything that is lingering and causing you residual pain should be put into this bubble so that you can let it go.

Once you are done putting all of the thoughts and images into the bubble, imagine that the dots connecting the bubble to your head fade away. Then, you can take a deep breath and blow at the bubble. Continue blowing it, as you blow it away from you. Eventually, it will get so far that it starts to fade away and you can no longer see it. Soon, it will completely fade and will be nothing but a distant, neutralized memory.

When you can no longer see the bubble, take a few moments to breathe deeply. Imagine that you are already living life free of any of the residual pain you were experiencing. Notice how much more free you feel when you are no longer a victim of the painful remnants of emotions. Take some time to say to yourself "I am free". Preferably, say it at least three times over. When you are done, smile and take a few more deep breaths. Then, you can stand up from the chair, exit the room and close the door firmly behind you. Walk one by one up each stair until you are at the top of the stairs. Then, you can take a few more deep breaths and open your eyes and return to the actual room that surrounds you. When you are ready, you can stretch out your limbs and prepare yourself to return to your daily life.

Releasing techniques are important because they can help eliminate emotional build up. Sometimes you will want to use releasing techniques in addition to addressing painful emotions because there is so much to work through. You won't always be able to work through everything in one or two sessions. Sometimes you will have to work through things a few times until you completely address all of the unwanted feelings and release everything.

If you are working through addressing painful emotions, you should always practice some form of release afterward. Releasing after each session is a way of gaining closure from the session. It essentially seals the deal. You might think of the process of addressing painful emotions as being the bleeding of a wound and then the process of releasing being your wound scabbing over. The healing process deepens when you properly release all of the residual build up around it.

Alternatively, some days you may experience a significant amount of negative energies. Stress may build up and as a result the negativity of your daily environment may affect you more than normal. If this happens, you will want to practice releasing as well. In this case, you are simply releasing unwanted energies. This is different from ignoring emotions as in this instance there are generally no real emotions to be released. Instead, you are simply releasing the build up after a particularly difficult day.

Releasing is a powerful technique that can be done in many ways. When you look around you may discover that there are hundreds, if not thousands of methods for you to release unwanted energies and emotions after you are done working through them. Some may give you the illusion that if you use the technique you can release unwanted emotions before you have effectively worked through them. Please take the time to note that this is untrue and is never possible. Any time you attempt to release unwanted emotions before working through them, you are merely suppressing them to be dealt with at a later time. There is virtually no way to run away from your emotions. You must deal with them at one time or another. The longer you wait, the harder it will be for you to work through it.

When Your Practice Fades

There comes a time in every mindfulness practitioner's life where their practice fades. This is completely natural. When you are busy in life, have a lot going on, or are struggling with difficult emotions or circumstances, it can be easy to negate away from your mindfulness practice. Sometimes you might think you will come back to it shortly, other times your mindfulness practice might appear as though it is the source of your pain. The specific reason as to why your practice has faded will determine how you can address the situation.

If your practice has faded because of a busy schedule or a lack of commitment, the best thing you can do is start at the beginning again. Head back to the "short strategies" section of this book and start practicing smaller sessions on a daily basis. Build yourself back up to the advanced strategy and then carry on as you were. You might find that you have to do this many times throughout your life as you may become busy and experience changes to your schedule that bump you off of your course. Simply restart and carry on and you will have effectively addressed this situation.

If your practice is fading because it no longer serves you in the way you need, you should spend some time addressing this issue. Notice where the practice was no longer serving you and adjust it so that it can begin to fulfill your needs once again. Occasionally we outgrow our mindfulness practices and if we don't adjust our practice we will simply discontinue it because we no longer feel we are gaining value from it. Never feel as though you need to stick to a specific routine or strategy in order to maintain your mindfulness practice. As you grow, you will likely feel natural pulls to adjust or alter it in certain ways. When you experience this, the best thing you can do is appreciate the tugs and follow them. More often than not, your intuition will be able to guide you in the way that will fill your needs the best.

Another thing that commonly draws people away from mindfulness practices is the difficult times. If you are experiencing difficult emotions, you may no longer want to practice your mindfulness techniques. Because mindfulness encourages you to face the difficulty, it can be easy to want to avoid it so that you don't have to feel the discomfort. If you have been avoiding your practice for this reason, it is extremely important that you don't hold yourself in contempt for it. There is no reason to feel as though you are in need of being punished because you are struggling to face a difficult emotion. Instead, gently guide yourself back into your mindfulness practice. You should start at the beginning by reintroducing the easier strategies into your practice again. As well, when you are ready, you will want to work through the strategies from this chapter. Getting to the root cause, addressing painful emotions and learning to release will all help you effectively work through the process of dealing with the emotions you have been struggling with and moving forward with your life and mindfulness practice. The more you are open to growth and change in your life, the more you will experience.

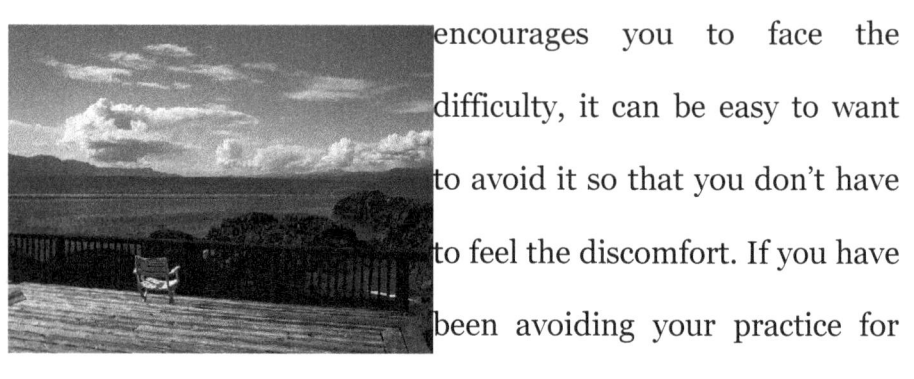

When your mindfulness practice begins to fade, it is always important that you accept that there is a natural ebb and flow to the practice. You won't always feel as though you are as committed as you once were. Sometimes you will feel more dedicated, other times you will feel less dedicated. Sometimes you may even forget to practice for several days at a time. There is no reason to feel guilty or shameful about these experiences. Instead, recognize that a true mindfulness practice is fluid and the way you feel and the way you work with it will vary from day to day. Many circumstances and factors go into the development of a mindfulness practice, you will simply need to take your time and be patient.

Something worth realizing is that when your mindfulness practices fades, this is generally a powerful opportunity for you to learn more about yourself. When you learn about why it has faded, you can explore that further and develop a greater sense of understanding as to why that was your response and what you can do about it that will genuinely work for you. The more you learn about yourself, the better. After all, that is what mindfulness is all about!

In your mindfulness journey, there will be times when the simple day-to-day maintenance is not enough. You will need to invest some more energy and focus into the development of your practice sometimes. When you are having particularly difficult emotions, are carrying around a large amount of stress, anxiety or depression, or when you are noticing your practice is not as strong as it once was, you will need to implement larger strategies.

These strategies are not ones that need to be used in your daily routine. However, you can and should use them as often as you need to in order to gain the appropriate benefits from them. If you are experiencing particularly large emotions that are difficult for you, it may take several days, weeks, or even months to work through those emotions. Take as long as you need and be gentle with yourself. When you are done, you will return to a place where you can manage your mindfulness with simpler daily routines. Take it easy and always have patience with yourself. The more gentle you are, the quicker you will adapt to your mindfulness practice and gain the benefits from it.

CONCLUSION

Mindfulness is a powerful practice for helping you eliminate stress, anxiety, depression, and other uncomfortable emotions. It is important to always recognize that mindfulness isn't a remedy for unwanted emotions, but rather it is an opportunity to work through those emotions in an effective way so that you can move past them. It is an indirect strategy for dealing with difficult emotions.

In your own mindfulness practice, you will be encouraged to learn more about yourself. The greater self-awareness you have, the more you will know exactly what you need in order to work through difficult emotions. It may not make it easier for you to work through them, however it will make you more aware as to how you will feel as you do. Ultimately, mindfulness is an exploration of your inner self that leads to a place where you can consciously work together with your emotions to generate a life of peace and happiness.

I hope this book was able to teach you several effective strategies for developing your own mindfulness practice. It is important to start by working up your short strategies and becoming used to them. While you may feel inclined to jump straight into a more advanced practice, the reality is that this is not beneficial. Working in this way can result in you getting in over your head and feeling overwhelmed, thus abandoning your practice and feeling reluctant to start over again. Start small, gain momentum and confidence, and then work your way up. Remember, if you struggle to maintain your practice, simply start over again and take it easy. If you are dealing with intense or difficult emotions, be sure to give yourself the opportunity to address them properly and then release them properly as well.

The next step is for you to start practicing the short strategies in your daily routine. Start small and master this stage first. Once you feel extremely confident in this level, you can move forward to start transitioning into the more advanced practice. Again, when you are transitioning you should still start small. Take it easy with the transition and make sure that you are only adding one part of the advanced strategy at a time. As you feel more confident in each part of the strategy, you can transition more and more until you have fully embraced the advanced level. Then, you can work on maintaining your mindfulness practice and evolving it in the way that feels best for you.

Lastly, if you enjoyed this book I ask that you please take the time to rate it on Amazon Kindle. Your honest review would be greatly appreciated.

Thank you!